CONTENTS

WHAT CAN ASTROLOGY
do for me?

Astrology is a powerful tool for self-awareness. The idea that we are all connected—that the shifting energies of the Sun, Moon, and planets above affect us here on Earth—is an ancient and philosophical belief. Astrology isn't fortune-telling—it can't predict your future and it doesn't deal in absolutes. It simply says that you are part of the universe around you, and by studying the stars, it's possible to learn more about yourself.

Why is this so important? Because the better understanding you have of your own inner makeup—your skills, your talents, your needs, and your fears—the more insight you gain into why you act the way you do. And this gives you choices, empowering you to make changes and to build on your strengths. It makes it easier to feel confident and to accept yourself, quirks and all.

There are countless daily horoscopes in newspapers, magazines, and online. But this book looks at more than just your star sign, which is only a small part of your personality picture. It helps you to find your Rising sign, which was appearing over the Eastern horizon at the time of your birth, and has a lot to tell you about the way others see you. You can also work out your Moon sign, which reveals the real you deep down inside, giving you the chance to get to grips with your innermost emotions, desires, fears, and obsessions.

With a clearer picture of who you are, life becomes less complicated. Instead of trying to live up to others' expectations and being someone you're not, you can work instead on becoming the best version of yourself possible—someone who understands their talents and needs, who is perfectly unique, and is happy.

What is
ASTROLOGY?

The stars and planets have always inspired a sense of wonder. The ancient peoples of Babylonia, Persia, Egypt, Greece, and India were all fascinated by the cycles of the Moon, the rising and setting of the Sun, the position of the constellations, and what it all meant. As these civilizations developed, they connected what they saw in the sky with the people and events on Earth, and astrology was born.

In ancient times, astrology was used to help monarchs rule. Kings and emperors would employ astrologers to predict the weather, speak to the gods, and help manage the country.

Modern astrology has evolved to help ordinary people like you and me understand ourselves better—how we behave, how we feel about each other, and how we can make the best of who we are.

THE SIGNS OF THE ZODIAC

Today we know that the planets revolve around the Sun, but astrology is based on how we see the solar system from here on Earth. The Zodiac is a group of 12 constellations that, from our viewpoint, seem to rotate around Earth over the course of a year, like a huge wheel. These constellations are named for the animals and objects that our ancestors thought they looked most like—the ram, the lion, the scorpion, and so on. Your Sun sign tells you which of the constellations the Sun was moving through on the day you were born. The signs have a natural order that never varies, beginning with Aries. The dates given on the right change slightly from year to year for the same reasons we have a leap year—each of our days is slightly longer than 24 hours. If you were born at the beginning or end of a sign, called "the cusp," it's worth checking your Sun sign online to be sure.

ARIES
March 21–April 20

TAURUS
April 21–May 21

GEMINI
May 22–June 21

CANCER
June 22–July 22

LEO
July 23–August 23

VIRGO
August 24–September 22

LIBRA
September 23–October 22

SCORPIO
October 23–November 21

SAGITTARIUS
November 22–December 21

CAPRICORN
December 22–January 20

AQUARIUS
January 21–February 19

PISCES
February 20–March 20

THE FOUR ELEMENTS

Each Sun sign is associated with one of four elements—
Fire, Earth, Air, and Water.

FIRE

Aries, Leo, Sagittarius
Fire signs are passionate, dynamic, and temperamental.
They mix well with: Fire and Air types

EARTH

Taurus, Virgo, Capricorn
Earth signs are practical, cautious, and reliable.
They mix well with: Water and Earth types

AIR

Gemini, Libra, Aquarius
Air signs are quick, curious, and adventurous.
They mix well with: Air and Fire types

WATER

Cancer, Scorpio, Pisces
Water signs are sensitive, emotional, and kind.
They mix well with: Earth and Water types

THE PLANETS

Astrology looks at the positions of the stars and planets at the time and place of your birth. The Sun and Moon aren't technically planets, but they're referred to that way by astrologers for ease of use. The Sun is a great place to start—it's the most important object in the solar system. Your Sun sign describes the essence of your identity and says a great deal about your potential—the person you might become.

The position the Moon held in the sky at the time of your birth has a strong influence, too. It describes your emotions—how you feel deep inside. It can give you a better understanding of what you need to feel loved and cared for.

And there's also your Rising sign. This is the sign of the Zodiac that was appearing over the Eastern horizon at the time of your birth. It tells you more about how you interact with the world around you, especially to new situations. It's the filter through which you perceive the world and the impression you give to others on first meeting. Which means it's also how others often see you.

The positions of the other planets—Venus, Mercury, Mars, etc.—in your birth chart all have their own effect. But these three taken together—Sun, Moon, and Rising sign—will give you a deeper understanding of who you are and what you could become, your strengths and weaknesses, your real self.

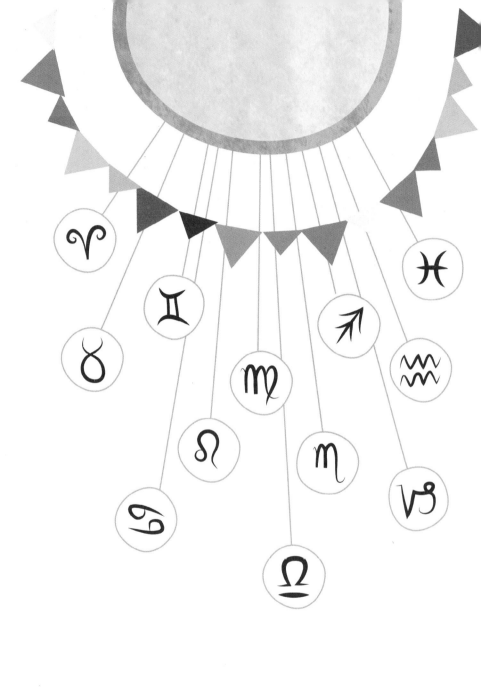

Your SUN sign

AQUARIUS

January 21–February 19

SYMBOL
The Water Bearer

ELEMENT
Air

RULING PLANET
Uranus

BIRTHSTONE
Amethyst

COLOR
Turquoise

BODY PART
Ankles, calves

DAY OF THE WEEK
Saturday

FLOWER
Orchid

CHARACTER TRAITS
Eccentric, independent, imaginative

KEY PHRASE
"I know"

YOUR SUN SIGN

When people talk about astrology and ask about your star sign, they're referring to your Sun sign. It tells you which of the 12 constellations of the Zodiac the Sun was moving through on the day you were born. This makes it easy to work out, which is one of the reasons for its popularity. If you'd like to know the Sun sign of a friend or family member, the table on page 7 shows which days the Sun occupies each of the signs over the course of a year.

The Sun is the heart of your chart—it's the essence of who you are and symbolizes the potential of what you can achieve. It's important to remember, though, that it is only a part of the whole picture when it comes to astrology. It's a wonderful starting point, but there are many other layers encasing your core identity, all of which affect the inner you.

ALL ABOUT YOU

Born with the Sun in Aquarius, you have the potential to shake things up and bring about change. One of your strongest traits is that you're an independent thinker. You don't just accept what you are told but come up with your own original conclusions. And it follows that your friends should have this open-mindedness, too. You have a small but super-close friendship circle because you are quite choosy about who you let into your world. For you, it's about quality, not quantity.

Even though you are a fixed sign (which normally means a love of stability), Aquarians are hooked on change. You absolutely need to live a life packed with adventure—boring routines are a big no-no.

That doesn't mean you're too wrapped up in your own stuff to lend a listening ear to a friend who might be struggling, though. In fact, because you really listen and use that independent mind of yours to see situations from a fresh angle, you're great at coming up with practical suggestions that actually work.

You're still likely to have your friends scratching their heads in confusion now and then. Why? Because no one can predict what you'll do next: one moment you're happy to be fully involved with everything, the next you're running off for some me-time. You don't really care about other people's expectations—you're happy doing your own thing.

Likes

Standing out
Conspiracy theories
Feeling unique
Space to think
Working together
Facts and figures

Dislikes

Rules
Being copied
Getting emotional

HOW TO BRING OUT YOUR BEST

You're exceptionally good at seeing the bigger picture—you can stand back and find patterns and links between things that are seemingly unrelated. Imaginative and original, you need space to get those creative juices flowing. This means there are times when you might want to give louder personalities in the world a pass. Although you love hanging out with your friends, if you have some kind of problem to deal with, you prefer to take yourself off to a place where you can hear yourself think.

The cogs of your brain rarely stop whirring and there's a danger you can overthink things, making yourself unnecessarily stressed. If you can identify the telltale signs—perhaps waking up in the night—you can try some distraction techniques like mindful coloring or a nature walk.

Strengths

Creative
Idealistic
Curious
Original
Quirky
Clever
Innovative

Weaknesses

Stubborn
Rebellious
Aloof

SECRET FEARS

Your symbol is the Water Bearer, the carrier of emotions. It's important you find ways to express your innermost feelings, whether that's through songwriting, poetry, art, or dance. However, you can have a thin skin at times, so you will worry about your work being criticized. These fears are generally unfounded, as your honesty is likely to connect deeply with people.

You are one of the Zodiac's most independent signs—a true free spirit—but you have an ever-present worry that one day you will have to fit in with the rest of the crowd to do well in life. Your more conventional friends might make you feel a bit like this. They are happy to follow the rules—but you're not! Sure, it might be a tougher path to take at times, but you have to remain true to yourself.

Most likely to . . .

Win the Nobel prize

Argue for the sake of it

Offer advice

Have cool hair

Feel above it all

Get along with anyone

Switch to a random topic

Be two steps ahead of everyone else

Your RISING sign

YOUR RISING SIGN

Your Rising sign, also known as your Ascendant, is the sign that was rising over the Eastern horizon (the place where the Sun rises each day) when you were born. It describes how you see the world and the people around you and how they see you—the first impression that you give and receive, the image you project, and the initial reaction you might have to a new situation. A person with Leo Rising, for example, may strike you as warm and engaging, whereas Pisces Rising is more sensitive and possibly shy. Because the Ascendant is determined by the exact time and place you were born, it is the most personal point in your chart. Many astrologers believe this makes it just as important as your Sun sign.

HOW TO FIND YOUR ASCENDANT

This is where it gets a bit tricky. There's a reason that popular astrology only deals with your Sun sign—your Rising sign can be more difficult to work out. But don't be put off. If you know your Sun sign and your time of birth, you can use the table on the right to give you a good idea. To be totally accurate you do need to take into account factors like time zone and daylight savings, and there are plenty of free online calculators that will do just that.

YOUR SUN SIGN	YOUR HOUR OF BIRTH											
	6:00 AM to 8:00 AM	8:00 AM to 10:00 AM	10:00 AM to 12:00 PM	12:00 PM to 2:00 PM	2:00 PM to 4:00 PM	4:00 PM to 6:00 PM	6:00 PM to 8:00 PM	8:00 PM to 10:00 PM	10:00 PM to 12:00 AM	12:00 AM to 2:00 AM	2:00 AM to 4:00 AM	4:00 AM to 6:00 AM
ARIES ♈	♉	♊	♋	♌	♍	♎	♏	♐	♑	♒	♓	♈
TAURUS ♉	♊	♋	♌	♍	♎	♏	♐	♑	♒	♓	♈	♉
GEMINI ♊	♋	♌	♍	♎	♏	♐	♑	♒	♓	♈	♉	♊
CANCER ♋	♌	♍	♎	♏	♐	♑	♒	♓	♈	♉	♊	♋
LEO ♌	♍	♎	♏	♐	♑	♒	♓	♈	♉	♊	♋	♌
VIRGO ♍	♎	♏	♐	♑	♒	♓	♈	♉	♊	♋	♌	♍
LIBRA ♎	♏	♐	♑	♒	♓	♈	♉	♊	♋	♌	♍	♎
SCORPIO ♏	♐	♑	♒	♓	♈	♉	♊	♋	♌	♍	♎	♏
SAGITTARIUS ♐	♑	♒	♓	♈	♉	♊	♋	♌	♍	♎	♏	♐
CAPRICORN ♑	♒	♓	♈	♉	♊	♋	♌	♍	♎	♏	♐	♑
AQUARIUS ♒	♓	♈	♉	♊	♋	♌	♍	♎	♏	♐	♑	♒
PISCES ♓	♈	♉	♊	♋	♌	♍	♎	♏	♐	♑	♒	♓

WHAT YOUR RISING SIGN SAYS ABOUT YOU

Once you have figured out your Ascendant, you are ready to discover more about how you see the world, and how it sees you.

ARIES RISING

The fire of Aries combines well with the air of Aquarius. You are the livewire of the bunch, bounding through life with an infectious energy. It's a wonder you don't need to hire a PA to manage your high school social life—you're super-popular with your classmates. And your forward-planning mentality makes you a star student because you usually hand in assignments days ahead of deadline. There's one thing to watch for, though. Always surging ahead means you might miss out on what's happening in the here and now. Bring yourself into the moment with some energizing deep breaths.

TAURUS RISING

The bull's legendary stubbornness can challenge even the most easygoing Aquarius. This means that when something gets too complicated for you to understand, you might shut down and not listen to what's being said. If you can lighten up and open your ears and mind to a new way of thinking, you might just find that life runs much more smoothly. Your generosity of spirit is one of your loveliest assets, and if you're considering making a future career in the charity sector, they would be very lucky to have you.

GEMINI RISING

When curious Gemini meets quick-minded Aquarius, the result is one of the Zodiac's most talkative signs. You hatch new ideas by the hour and can't resist sharing them with anyone in close range. While it may get a little wearing for your friends on occasion, they are probably hugely entertained by some of your more "out there" schemes. With your sharp mind, you can love an argument for the sake of it—the trick is to know when you're pushing it too far.

CANCER RISING

Cautious Cancer can hold back the outgoing Aquarius if not kept in check. You may have a fear of rejection that stops you from expressing yourself fully. When this happens, reach out to a friend and ask them to remind you why they love to hang out with you. This will help to boost your confidence and to share what's on your mind. Aquarians tend to be pretty enlightened souls, so you'll probably amaze and delight people with your ideas.

LEO RISING

When Leo joins forces with Aquarius, there's more than a touch of drama! You have a big personality that can sometimes overshadow your friends, so it's important to let them have their moment in the sun, too. After all, you can channel all of that buzzing energy into your high school's drama club. And as an adult, you may find you turn to acting or stand-up comedy as your chosen career. Bear in mind that Leo strength can make you feel invincible and may lead you into a tight spot. Scope out a situation first before jumping in, and you'll be okay.

VIRGO RISING

This is a dynamic pairing. Aquarians with Virgo as their Rising sign are always looking for ways to improve things. It's not about seeking applause for your efforts, either: you get satisfaction from the process. Your friends may have to reassure you from time to time, however, because you can lose your confidence unexpectedly. As a student, you're likely to be on the soccer team or sign up to help out at the school bake sale. And this team-player spirit will spill over into your adult life when you join a new company and waste no time helping out your colleagues.

LIBRA RISING

When Libra's obliging nature meets the wonderful openness of those born under Aquarius, you're one of the most easygoing people to be around. You'll bend over backward to help out those you love, and before you know it, there's precious little time left to pursue your own dreams. Therefore, be mindful of this tendency and carve out space in your day just for you. You have a cool head in stressful situations, so in your future working life, you'll be an asset in any professions that require quick, clear thinking.

SCORPIO RISING

This partnership makes for an intense personality. You are always on your toes, ready for anything—in fact, you can be overly suspicious of other people's motives. If you can channel that energy into following your own path, the sky's the limit. Often preoccupied and with a set agenda, you don't appreciate being disrupted. You have an equal mix of practical know-how and technological wizardry to turn your hand to invention. Of course, not all of your bright ideas will fly, but you'll love the process of trying!

SAGITTARIUS RISING

Aquarius is already a highly intelligent sign, and when Sagittarius joins the party, you may well be one of the brightest students in class. You're no show-off, so your friends won't feel intimidated—your biggest problem will be having plenty of excuses ready when they ask you to do their assignments for them! An appreciation of beauty and design could lead to an architecture career: you've certainly got the smarts required.

CAPRICORN RISING

The Capricorn influence brings with it a hard-working attitude. So, you're likely to be the last student in the library, studying into the night to do well in your high school exams. In fact, you apply this go-getting energy to most aspects of your life, although your friendships can sometimes fall by the wayside if you're not careful. Remember that everyone needs some fun in their life if you start getting too serious. It's important to learn how to switch off for your overall well-being.

AQUARIUS RISING

With double Aquarius, you have a magnetic personality that attracts friends like a moth to a flame. As well as being a natural comic, you have a kind soul: your mantra is, "Do unto others as you'd have them do unto you." With your ability to find common ground with almost anyone you meet, your passage through life will flow with ease. Behind your laid-back exterior, you have a natural "alertness"—in adulthood, you may harness this in professions such as emergency services or airplane pilot.

PISCES RISING

Your sixth sense is heightened with this combination. You're an original thinker, too, so if a friend has something on their mind, you can often come up with a solution they wouldn't have thought of. However, while you may be totally "zen" on the outside, you can do a good job of hiding your own anxieties. Joining a meditation class may help you get these different sides in sync, and you can ground yourself when necessary by kicking off your shoes and feeling the earth beneath your feet.

Your MOON sign

YOUR MOON SIGN

The Moon rules your emotions and your inner moods, telling you what you need to feel safe, comfortable, and loved. Knowing your Moon sign should give you a more complete picture of your unique self, helping you to express needs you might be struggling to understand. Suppose your Sun sign is Aries but being first has never been important to you—a Moon in Virgo may be telling you to hang back and fade into the background. Or you might have the Sun in home-loving Cancer but feel an urge to get out there and see the world. Perhaps that's because your Moon is in freedom-loving Sagittarius.

HOW TO FIND YOUR MOON SIGN

Just like your Rising sign, finding your Moon sign is more complicated than finding your Sun sign. That's because the Moon seems to move so quickly, taking just about a month to pass through all of the constellations. Thankfully, the tables on the right and on the next page make finding it a simple process.

First, find your year of birth. Then locate your birth month at the top of the table. Find your date of birth in the column below it, and this will give you your Moon sign. If your date of birth isn't listed, the one before it is your Moon sign.

For example, suppose your date of birth is March 4, 1995. The date before this is March 2, for which the Moon sign is Aries. This would mean your Moon sign is Aries.

JAN	FEB	MAR	APR	MAY	JUN	JUL	AUG	SEP	OCT	NOV	DEC

BORN IN THE YEAR 1995

JAN	FEB	MAR	APR	MAY	JUN	JUL	AUG	SEP	OCT	NOV	DEC
2 Aqu	1 Pis	2 Ari	1 Tau	1 Gem	2 Leo	2 Vir	3 Sco	1 Sag	2 Aqu	1 Pis	3 Tau
4 Pis	3 Ari	5 Tau	3 Gem	3 Can	5 Vir	4 Lib	5 Sag	3 Cap	5 Pis	3 Ari	5 Gem
7 Ari	5 Tau	7 Gem	6 Can	6 Leo	7 Lib	6 Sco	7 Cap	5 Aqu	7 Ari	5 Tau	8 Can
9 Tau	8 Gem	10 Can	9 Leo	8 Vir	9 Sco	8 Sag	9 Aqu	7 Pis	9 Tau	8 Gem	10 Leo
12 Gem	10 Can	12 Leo	11 Vir	10 Lib	11 Sag	10 Cap	11 Pis	9 Ari	12 Gem	10 Can	13 Vir
14 Can	13 Leo	14 Vir	13 Lib	13 Sco	13 Cap	12 Aqu	13 Ari	12 Tau	14 Can	13 Leo	15 Lib
16 Leo	15 Vir	17 Lib	15 Sco	15 Sag	15 Aqu	14 Pis	15 Tau	14 Gem	17 Leo	15 Vir	17 Sco
19 Vir	17 Lib	19 Sco	17 Sag	17 Cap	17 Pis	17 Ari	18 Gem	17 Can	19 Vir	18 Lib	19 Sag
21 Lib	19 Sco	21 Sag	19 Cap	19 Aqu	19 Ari	19 Tau	20 Can	19 Leo	21 Lib	20 Sco	21 Cap
23 Sco	22 Sag	23 Cap	21 Aqu	21 Pis	22 Tau	22 Gem	23 Leo	22 Vir	23 Sco	22 Sag	23 Aqu
25 Sag	24 Cap	25 Aqu	24 Pis	23 Ari	24 Gem	24 Can	25 Vir	24 Lib	26 Sag	24 Cap	25 Pis
27 Cap	26 Aqu	27 Pis	26 Ari	26 Tau	27 Can	27 Leo	28 Lib	26 Sco	28 Cap	26 Aqu	28 Ari
30 Aqu	28 Pis	30 Ari	28 Tau	28 Gem	29 Leo	29 Vir	30 Sco	28 Sag	30 Aqu	28 Pis	30 Tau
				31 Can		31 Lib		30 Cap		30 Ari	

BORN IN THE YEAR 1996

JAN	FEB	MAR	APR	MAY	JUN	JUL	AUG	SEP	OCT	NOV	DEC
1 Gem	3 Leo	1 Leo	2 Lib	2 Sco	2 Cap	2 Aqu	2 Ari	1 Tau	3 Can	2 Leo	2 Vir
4 Can	5 Vir	3 Vir	4 Sco	4 Sag	4 Aqu	4 Pis	4 Tau	3 Gem	5 Leo	4 Vir	4 Lib
6 Leo	8 Lib	6 Lib	7 Sag	6 Cap	6 Pis	6 Ari	7 Gem	6 Can	8 Vir	7 Lib	6 Sco
9 Vir	10 Sco	8 Sco	9 Cap	8 Aqu	9 Ari	8 Tau	9 Can	8 Leo	10 Lib	9 Sco	9 Sag
11 Lib	12 Sag	10 Sag	11 Aqu	10 Pis	11 Tau	11 Gem	12 Leo	11 Vir	13 Sco	11 Sag	11 Cap
14 Sco	15 Cap	12 Cap	13 Pis	12 Ari	13 Gem	13 Can	14 Vir	13 Lib	15 Sag	13 Cap	13 Aqu
16 Sag	16 Aqu	15 Aqu	15 Ari	15 Tau	16 Can	16 Leo	17 Lib	15 Sco	17 Cap	16 Aqu	15 Pis
18 Cap	18 Pis	17 Pis	17 Tau	17 Gem	18 Leo	18 Vir	19 Sco	18 Sag	19 Aqu	18 Pis	17 Ari
20 Aqu	20 Ari	19 Ari	20 Gem	19 Can	21 Vir	21 Lib	21 Sag	20 Cap	21 Pis	20 Ari	19 Tau
22 Pis	23 Tau	21 Tau	22 Can	22 Leo	23 Lib	23 Sco	24 Cap	22 Aqu	23 Ari	22 Tau	22 Gem
24 Ari	25 Gem	23 Gem	25 Leo	25 Vir	26 Sco	25 Sag	26 Aqu	24 Pis	26 Tau	24 Gem	24 Can
26 Tau	27 Can	26 Can	27 Vir	28 Sag	28 Sag	27 Cap	28 Pis	26 Ari	28 Gem	27 Can	26 Leo
29 Gem		28 Leo	30 Lib	29 Sco	30 Cap	29 Aqu	30 Ari	28 Tau	30 Can	29 Leo	29 Vir
31 Can		31 Vir		31 Sag		31 Pis		30 Gem			31 Lib

BORN IN THE YEAR 1997

JAN	FEB	MAR	APR	MAY	JUN	JUL	AUG	SEP	OCT	NOV	DEC
3 Sco	1 Sag	1 Sag	1 Aqu	1 Pis	1 Tau	1 Gem	2 Leo	3 Lib	3 Sco	1 Sag	1 Cap
5 Sag	4 Cap	3 Cap	3 Ari	3 Ari	4 Gem	3 Can	4 Vir	6 Sco	5 Sag	4 Cap	3 Aqu
7 Cap	6 Aqu	5 Aqu	6 Ari	5 Tau	6 Can	5 Leo	7 Lib	8 Sag	8 Cap	6 Aqu	5 Pis
9 Aqu	8 Pis	7 Pis	8 Tau	7 Gem	8 Leo	8 Vir	9 Sco	10 Cap	10 Aqu	8 Pis	8 Ari
11 Pis	10 Ari	9 Ari	10 Gem	9 Can	11 Vir	10 Lib	12 Sag	12 Aqu	12 Pis	10 Ari	10 Tau
13 Ari	12 Tau	11 Tau	12 Can	12 Leo	13 Lib	13 Sco	14 Cap	15 Pis	14 Ari	12 Tau	12 Gem
15 Tau	14 Gem	13 Gem	14 Leo	14 Vir	16 Sco	15 Sag	16 Aqu	17 Ari	16 Tau	14 Gem	14 Can
18 Gem	16 Can	16 Can	17 Vir	17 Lib	18 Sag	18 Cap	18 Pis	19 Tau	18 Gem	17 Can	16 Leo
20 Can	19 Leo	18 Leo	19 Lib	19 Sco	20 Cap	20 Aqu	20 Ari	21 Gem	20 Can	19 Leo	19 Vir
23 Leo	21 Vir	21 Vir	22 Sco	22 Sag	22 Aqu	22 Pis	22 Tau	23 Can	23 Leo	21 Vir	21 Lib
25 Vir	24 Lib	23 Lib	24 Sag	24 Cap	24 Pis	24 Ari	24 Gem	25 Leo	25 Vir	24 Lib	24 Sco
28 Lib	26 Sco	26 Sco	27 Cap	26 Aqu	26 Ari	26 Tau	27 Can	28 Vir	28 Lib	26 Sco	26 Sag
30 Sco		28 Sag	29 Aqu	28 Pis	29 Tau	28 Gem	29 Leo	30 Lib	30 Sco	29 Sag	28 Cap
		30 Cap		30 Ari		30 Can	31 Vir				31 Aqu

BORN IN THE YEAR 1998

JAN	FEB	MAR	APR	MAY	JUN	JUL	AUG	SEP	OCT	NOV	DEC
2 Pis	2 Tau	2 Tau	2 Can	2 Leo	3 Lib	3 Sco	2 Sag	3 Aqu	2 Pis	1 Ari	2 Gem
4 Ari	4 Gem	4 Gem	4 Leo	4 Vir	5 Sco	5 Sag	4 Cap	5 Pis	4 Ari	3 Tau	4 Can
6 Tau	7 Can	6 Can	7 Vir	7 Lib	8 Sag	8 Cap	6 Aqu	7 Ari	6 Tau	5 Gem	6 Leo
8 Gem	9 Leo	8 Leo	9 Lib	9 Sco	10 Cap	10 Aqu	8 Pis	9 Tau	8 Gem	7 Can	9 Vir
10 Can	11 Vir	11 Vir	12 Sco	12 Sag	13 Aqu	12 Pis	11 Ari	11 Gem	10 Can	9 Leo	11 Lib
13 Leo	14 Lib	13 Lib	14 Sag	14 Cap	15 Pis	14 Ari	13 Tau	13 Can	13 Leo	11 Vir	14 Sco
15 Vir	16 Sco	16 Sco	17 Cap	16 Aqu	17 Ari	16 Tau	15 Gem	15 Leo	15 Vir	14 Lib	16 Sag
18 Lib	19 Sag	18 Sag	19 Aqu	19 Pis	19 Tau	18 Gem	17 Can	18 Vir	17 Lib	16 Sco	19 Cap
20 Sco	21 Cap	21 Cap	21 Pis	21 Ari	21 Gem	21 Can	19 Leo	20 Lib	20 Sco	19 Sag	21 Aqu
23 Sag	23 Aqu	23 Aqu	23 Ari	23 Tau	23 Can	23 Leo	21 Vir	23 Sco	23 Sag	21 Cap	23 Pis
25 Cap	25 Pis	25 Pis	25 Tau	25 Gem	25 Leo	25 Vir	24 Lib	25 Sag	25 Cap	24 Aqu	25 Ari
27 Aqu	27 Ari	27 Ari	27 Gem	27 Can	28 Vir	28 Lib	26 Sco	28 Cap	27 Aqu	26 Pis	28 Tau
29 Pis		29 Tau	29 Can	29 Leo	30 Lib	30 Sco	29 Sag	30 Aqu	30 Pis	28 Ari	30 Gem
31 Ari		31 Gem		31 Vir			31 Cap			30 Tau	

BORN IN THE YEAR 1999

JAN	FEB	MAR	APR	MAY	JUN	JUL	AUG	SEP	OCT	NOV	DEC
1 Can	1 Vir	1 Vir	2 Sco	2 Sag	3 Aqu	2 Pis	1 Ari	2 Gem	1 Can	1 Vir	1 Lib
3 Leo	4 Lib	3 Lib	4 Sag	4 Cap	5 Pis	5 Ari	3 Tau	4 Can	3 Leo	4 Lib	3 Sco
5 Vir	6 Sco	6 Sco	7 Cap	7 Aqu	8 Ari	7 Tau	5 Gem	6 Leo	5 Vir	6 Sco	6 Sag
7 Lib	9 Sag	8 Sag	9 Aqu	9 Pis	10 Tau	9 Gem	7 Can	8 Vir	8 Lib	9 Sag	8 Cap
10 Sco	11 Cap	11 Cap	12 Pis	11 Ari	12 Gem	11 Can	9 Leo	10 Lib	10 Sco	11 Cap	11 Aqu
12 Sag	14 Aqu	13 Aqu	14 Ari	13 Tau	14 Can	13 Leo	12 Vir	13 Sco	12 Sag	14 Aqu	13 Pis
15 Cap	16 Pis	15 Pis	16 Tau	15 Gem	16 Leo	15 Vir	14 Lib	15 Sag	15 Cap	16 Pis	16 Ari
17 Aqu	18 Ari	17 Ari	18 Gem	17 Can	18 Vir	17 Lib	16 Sco	18 Cap	17 Aqu	18 Ari	18 Tau
19 Pis	20 Tau	19 Tau	20 Can	19 Leo	20 Lib	20 Sco	19 Sag	20 Aqu	20 Pis	21 Tau	20 Gem
22 Ari	22 Gem	21 Gem	22 Leo	21 Vir	23 Sco	22 Sag	21 Cap	22 Pis	22 Ari	23 Gem	22 Can
24 Tau	24 Can	23 Can	24 Vir	24 Lib	25 Sag	25 Cap	24 Aqu	25 Ari	24 Tau	25 Can	24 Leo
26 Gem	26 Leo	26 Leo	27 Lib	26 Sco	28 Cap	27 Aqu	26 Pis	27 Tau	26 Gem	27 Leo	26 Vir
28 Can		28 Vir	29 Sco	29 Sag	30 Aqu	30 Pis	28 Ari	29 Gem	28 Can	29 Vir	28 Lib
30 Leo		30 Lib		31 Cap			30 Tau		30 Leo		31 Sco

BORN IN THE YEAR 2000

JAN	FEB	MAR	APR	MAY	JUN	JUL	AUG	SEP	OCT	NOV	DEC
3 Sag	1 Cap	2 Aqu	1 Pis	3 Tau	1 Gem	2 Leo	1 Vir	2 Sco	1 Sag	3 Aqu	2 Pis
5 Cap	4 Aqu	4 Pis	3 Ari	5 Gem	3 Can	4 Vir	3 Lib	4 Sag	4 Cap	5 Pis	5 Ari
7 Aqu	6 Pis	6 Ari	5 Tau	7 Can	5 Leo	6 Lib	5 Sco	6 Cap	6 Aqu	8 Ari	7 Tau
10 Pis	8 Ari	9 Tau	7 Gem	9 Leo	7 Vir	9 Sco	8 Sag	9 Aqu	9 Pis	10 Tau	9 Gem
12 Ari	11 Tau	11 Gem	9 Can	11 Vir	9 Lib	11 Sag	10 Cap	11 Pis	11 Ari	12 Gem	11 Can
14 Tau	13 Gem	13 Can	11 Leo	13 Lib	12 Sco	14 Cap	13 Aqu	13 Ari	13 Tau	14 Can	13 Leo
16 Gem	15 Can	15 Leo	14 Vir	15 Sco	14 Sag	16 Aqu	15 Pis	16 Tau	16 Gem	16 Leo	15 Vir
18 Can	17 Leo	17 Vir	16 Lib	18 Sag	16 Cap	19 Pis	18 Ari	18 Gem	18 Can	18 Vir	18 Lib
20 Leo	19 Vir	20 Lib	18 Sco	20 Cap	19 Aqu	21 Ari	20 Tau	20 Can	20 Leo	20 Lib	20 Sco
23 Vir	21 Lib	22 Sco	21 Sag	23 Aqu	22 Pis	24 Tau	22 Gem	23 Leo	22 Vir	23 Sco	22 Sag
25 Lib	23 Sco	24 Sag	23 Cap	25 Pis	24 Ari	26 Gem	24 Can	25 Vir	24 Lib	25 Sag	25 Cap
27 Sco	26 Sag	27 Cap	26 Aqu	28 Ari	26 Tau	28 Can	26 Leo	27 Lib	27 Sco	27 Cap	27 Aqu
29 Sag	28 Cap	29 Aqu	28 Pis	30 Tau	28 Gem	30 Leo	28 Vir	29 Sco	29 Sag	30 Aqu	30 Pis
			30 Ari		30 Can		30 Lib		31 Cap		

BORN IN THE YEAR 2001

JAN	FEB	MAR	APR	MAY	JUN	JUL	AUG	SEP	OCT	NOV	DEC
1 Ari	2 Gem	1 Gem	2 Leo	1 Vir	2 Sco	1 Sag	3 Aqu	1 Pis	1 Ari	2 Gem	2 Can
4 Tau	4 Can	4 Can	4 Vir	3 Lib	4 Sag	4 Cap	5 Pis	4 Ari	4 Tau	4 Can	4 Leo
6 Gem	6 Leo	6 Leo	6 Lib	5 Sco	7 Cap	6 Aqu	8 Ari	6 Tau	6 Gem	7 Leo	6 Vir
8 Can	8 Vir	8 Vir	8 Sco	8 Sag	9 Aqu	9 Pis	10 Tau	9 Gem	8 Can	9 Vir	8 Lib
10 Leo	10 Lib	10 Lib	10 Sag	10 Cap	11 Pis	11 Ari	12 Gem	11 Can	10 Leo	11 Lib	10 Sco
12 Vir	12 Sco	12 Sco	13 Cap	13 Aqu	14 Ari	14 Tau	15 Can	13 Leo	13 Vir	13 Sco	12 Sag
14 Lib	15 Sag	14 Sag	15 Aqu	15 Pis	16 Tau	16 Gem	17 Leo	15 Vir	15 Lib	15 Sag	15 Cap
16 Sco	17 Cap	16 Cap	18 Pis	18 Ari	19 Gem	18 Can	19 Vir	17 Lib	17 Sco	17 Cap	17 Aqu
18 Sag	20 Aqu	19 Aqu	20 Ari	20 Tau	21 Can	20 Leo	21 Lib	19 Sco	19 Sag	20 Aqu	20 Pis
21 Cap	22 Pis	22 Pis	23 Tau	22 Gem	23 Leo	22 Vir	23 Sco	21 Sag	21 Cap	22 Pis	22 Ari
23 Aqu	25 Ari	24 Ari	25 Gem	24 Can	25 Vir	24 Lib	25 Sag	24 Cap	23 Aqu	25 Ari	25 Tau
26 Pis	27 Tau	26 Tau	27 Can	27 Leo	27 Lib	26 Sco	27 Cap	26 Aqu	26 Pis	27 Tau	27 Gem
28 Ari		29 Gem	29 Leo	29 Vir	29 Sco	29 Sag	30 Aqu	29 Pis	28 Ari	30 Gem	29 Can
31 Tau		31 Can		31 Lib		31 Cap			31 Tau		31 Leo

BORN IN THE YEAR 2002

JAN	FEB	MAR	APR	MAY	JUN	JUL	AUG	SEP	OCT	NOV	DEC
2 Vir	1 Lib	2 Sco	1 Sag	2 Aqu	1 Pis	1 Ari	2 Gem	1 Can	1 Leo	1 Lib	1 Sco
4 Lib	3 Sco	4 Sag	3 Cap	5 Pis	4 Ari	4 Tau	5 Can	3 Leo	3 Vir	3 Sco	3 Sag
6 Sco	5 Sag	6 Cap	5 Aqu	7 Ari	6 Tau	6 Gem	7 Leo	5 Vir	5 Lib	5 Sag	5 Cap
9 Sag	7 Cap	9 Aqu	8 Pis	10 Tau	9 Gem	9 Can	9 Vir	7 Lib	7 Sco	7 Cap	7 Aqu
11 Cap	10 Aqu	11 Pis	10 Ari	12 Gem	11 Can	11 Leo	11 Lib	9 Sco	9 Sag	10 Aqu	9 Pis
13 Aqu	12 Pis	14 Ari	13 Tau	15 Can	13 Leo	13 Vir	13 Sco	12 Sag	11 Cap	12 Pis	12 Ari
16 Pis	15 Ari	16 Tau	15 Gem	17 Leo	15 Vir	15 Lib	15 Sag	14 Cap	13 Aqu	15 Ari	14 Tau
18 Ari	17 Tau	19 Gem	18 Can	19 Vir	18 Lib	17 Sco	18 Cap	16 Aqu	16 Pis	17 Tau	17 Gem
21 Tau	20 Gem	21 Can	20 Leo	21 Lib	20 Sco	19 Sag	20 Aqu	19 Pis	18 Ari	20 Gem	19 Can
23 Gem	22 Can	24 Leo	22 Vir	23 Sco	22 Sag	22 Cap	22 Pis	21 Ari	21 Tau	22 Can	22 Leo
26 Can	24 Leo	26 Vir	24 Lib	25 Sag	24 Cap	24 Aqu	25 Ari	24 Tau	23 Gem	24 Leo	24 Vir
28 Leo	26 Vir	28 Lib	26 Sco	28 Cap	26 Aqu	26 Pis	27 Tau	26 Gem	26 Can	27 Vir	26 Lib
30 Vir	28 Lib	30 Sco	28 Sag	30 Aqu	29 Pis	28 Ari	30 Gem	29 Can	28 Leo	29 Lib	28 Sco
			30 Cap			31 Tau			30 Vir		30 Sag

JAN	FEB	MAR	APR	MAY	JUN	JUL	AUG	SEP	OCT	NOV	DEC
1 Cap	2 Pis	1 Pis	3 Tau	2 Gem	1 Can	1 Leo	2 Lib	2 Sag	1 Cap	2 Pis	2 Ari
3 Aqu	5 Ari	4 Ari	5 Gem	5 Can	4 Leo	3 Vir	4 Sco	4 Cap	4 Aqu	5 Ari	4 Tau
6 Pis	7 Tau	6 Tau	8 Can	7 Leo	6 Vir	5 Lib	6 Sag	6 Aqu	6 Pis	7 Tau	7 Gem
8 Ari	10 Gem	9 Gem	10 Leo	10 Vir	8 Lib	7 Sco	8 Cap	9 Pis	8 Ari	10 Gem	9 Can
11 Tau	12 Can	11 Can	12 Vir	12 Lib	10 Sco	10 Sag	10 Aqu	11 Ari	11 Tau	12 Can	12 Leo
13 Gem	14 Leo	14 Leo	14 Lib	14 Sco	12 Sag	12 Cap	12 Pis	13 Tau	13 Gem	15 Leo	14 Vir
16 Can	16 Vir	16 Vir	16 Sco	16 Sag	14 Cap	14 Aqu	15 Ari	16 Gem	16 Can	17 Vir	16 Lib
18 Leo	18 Lib	18 Lib	18 Sag	18 Cap	16 Aqu	16 Pis	17 Tau	18 Can	18 Leo	19 Lib	19 Sco
20 Vir	21 Sco	20 Sco	20 Cap	20 Aqu	19 Pis	18 Ari	20 Gem	21 Leo	21 Vir	21 Sco	21 Sag
22 Lib	23 Sag	22 Sag	23 Aqu	22 Pis	21 Ari	21 Tau	22 Can	23 Vir	23 Lib	23 Sag	23 Cap
24 Sco	25 Cap	24 Cap	25 Pis	25 Ari	23 Tau	23 Gem	24 Leo	25 Lib	25 Sco	25 Cap	25 Aqu
26 Sag	27 Aqu	26 Aqu	27 Ari	27 Tau	26 Gem	26 Can	27 Vir	27 Sco	27 Sag	27 Aqu	27 Pis
29 Cap		29 Pis	30 Tau	30 Gem	28 Can	28 Leo	29 Lib	29 Sag	29 Cap	29 Pis	29 Ari
31 Aqu		31 Ari				30 Vir	31 Sco		31 Aqu		

JAN	FEB	MAR	APR	MAY	JUN	JUL	AUG	SEP	OCT	NOV	DEC
1 Tau	2 Can	3 Leo	1 Vir	1 Lib	2 Sag	1 Cap	1 Pis	2 Tau	2 Gem	1 Can	1 Leo
3 Gem	4 Leo	5 Vir	4 Lib	3 Sco	4 Cap	3 Aqu	4 Ari	5 Gem	5 Can	3 Leo	3 Vir
6 Can	7 Vir	7 Lib	6 Sco	5 Sag	6 Aqu	5 Pis	6 Tau	7 Can	7 Leo	6 Vir	6 Lib
8 Leo	9 Lib	9 Sco	8 Sag	7 Cap	8 Pis	7 Ari	8 Gem	10 Leo	10 Vir	8 Lib	8 Sco
10 Vir	11 Sco	12 Sag	10 Cap	9 Aqu	10 Ari	10 Tau	11 Can	12 Vir	12 Lib	10 Sco	10 Sag
13 Lib	13 Sag	14 Cap	12 Aqu	11 Pis	12 Tau	12 Gem	13 Leo	14 Lib	14 Sco	12 Sag	12 Cap
15 Sco	15 Cap	16 Aqu	14 Pis	14 Ari	15 Gem	15 Can	16 Vir	17 Sco	16 Sag	15 Cap	14 Aqu
17 Sag	17 Aqu	18 Pis	16 Ari	16 Tau	17 Can	17 Leo	18 Lib	19 Sag	18 Cap	17 Aqu	16 Pis
19 Cap	20 Pis	20 Ari	19 Tau	19 Gem	20 Leo	20 Vir	20 Sco	21 Cap	20 Aqu	19 Pis	18 Ari
21 Aqu	22 Ari	23 Tau	21 Gem	21 Can	22 Vir	22 Lib	23 Sag	23 Aqu	23 Pis	21 Ari	21 Tau
23 Pis	24 Tau	25 Gem	24 Can	24 Leo	25 Lib	24 Sco	25 Cap	25 Pis	25 Ari	23 Tau	23 Gem
25 Ari	27 Gem	28 Can	26 Leo	26 Vir	27 Sco	26 Sag	27 Aqu	27 Ari	27 Tau	26 Gem	25 Can
28 Tau	29 Can	30 Leo	29 Vir	28 Lib	29 Sag	28 Cap	29 Pis	30 Tau	29 Gem	28 Can	28 Leo
30 Gem				31 Sco		30 Aqu	31 Ari				31 Vir

JAN	FEB	MAR	APR	MAY	JUN	JUL	AUG	SEP	OCT	NOV	DEC
2 Lib	1 Sco	2 Sag	3 Aqu	2 Pis	3 Tau	2 Gem	1 Can	2 Vir	2 Lib	1 Sco	2 Cap
4 Sco	3 Sag	4 Cap	5 Pis	4 Ari	5 Gem	5 Can	3 Leo	5 Lib	4 Sco	3 Sag	4 Aqu
6 Sag	5 Cap	6 Aqu	7 Ari	6 Tau	7 Can	7 Leo	6 Vir	7 Sco	7 Sag	5 Cap	7 Pis
8 Cap	7 Aqu	8 Pis	9 Tau	9 Gem	10 Leo	10 Vir	8 Lib	9 Sag	9 Cap	7 Aqu	9 Ari
10 Aqu	9 Pis	10 Ari	11 Gem	11 Can	12 Vir	12 Lib	11 Sco	12 Cap	11 Aqu	9 Pis	11 Tau
12 Pis	11 Ari	13 Tau	14 Can	14 Leo	15 Lib	15 Sco	13 Sag	14 Aqu	13 Pis	11 Ari	13 Gem
15 Ari	13 Tau	15 Gem	16 Leo	16 Vir	17 Sco	17 Sag	15 Cap	16 Pis	15 Ari	14 Tau	15 Can
17 Tau	16 Gem	17 Can	19 Vir	18 Lib	19 Sag	19 Cap	17 Aqu	18 Ari	17 Tau	16 Gem	18 Leo
19 Gem	18 Can	20 Leo	21 Lib	21 Sco	21 Cap	21 Aqu	19 Pis	20 Tau	19 Gem	18 Can	20 Vir
22 Can	21 Leo	22 Vir	23 Sco	23 Sag	23 Aqu	23 Pis	21 Ari	22 Gem	22 Can	21 Leo	23 Lib
24 Leo	23 Vir	25 Lib	26 Sag	25 Cap	25 Pis	25 Ari	23 Tau	24 Can	24 Leo	23 Vir	25 Sco
27 Vir	25 Lib	27 Sco	28 Cap	27 Aqu	28 Ari	27 Tau	26 Gem	27 Leo	27 Vir	26 Lib	28 Sag
29 Lib	28 Sco	29 Sag	30 Aqu	29 Pis	30 Tau	29 Gem	28 Can	29 Vir	29 Lib	28 Sco	30 Cap
		31 Cap		31 Ari			31 Leo			30 Sag	

JAN	FEB	MAR	APR	MAY	JUN	JUL	AUG	SEP	OCT	NOV	DEC
1 Aqu	1 Ari	1 Ari	1 Gem	1 Can	2 Vir	2 Lib	1 Sco	2 Cap	1 Aqu	2 Ari	1 Tau
3 Pis	3 Tau	3 Tau	4 Can	3 Leo	5 Lib	5 Sco	3 Sag	4 Aqu	4 Pis	4 Tau	3 Gem
5 Ari	6 Gem	5 Gem	6 Leo	6 Vir	7 Sco	7 Sag	6 Cap	6 Pis	6 Ari	6 Gem	6 Can
7 Tau	8 Can	7 Can	9 Vir	8 Lib	10 Sag	9 Cap	8 Aqu	8 Ari	8 Tau	8 Can	8 Leo
9 Gem	10 Leo	10 Leo	11 Lib	11 Sco	12 Cap	11 Aqu	10 Pis	10 Tau	10 Gem	10 Leo	10 Vir
12 Can	13 Vir	12 Vir	14 Sco	13 Sag	14 Aqu	13 Pis	12 Ari	12 Gem	12 Can	13 Vir	13 Lib
14 Leo	16 Lib	15 Lib	16 Sag	15 Cap	16 Pis	15 Ari	14 Tau	14 Can	14 Leo	15 Lib	15 Sco
17 Vir	18 Sco	17 Sco	18 Cap	18 Aqu	18 Ari	17 Tau	16 Gem	17 Leo	17 Vir	18 Sco	18 Sag
19 Lib	20 Sag	20 Sag	20 Aqu	20 Pis	20 Tau	19 Gem	18 Can	19 Vir	19 Lib	20 Sag	20 Cap
22 Sco	22 Cap	22 Cap	22 Pis	22 Ari	22 Gem	21 Can	21 Leo	22 Lib	22 Sco	23 Cap	22 Aqu
24 Sag	25 Aqu	24 Aqu	25 Ari	24 Tau	25 Can	24 Leo	23 Vir	24 Sco	24 Sag	25 Aqu	24 Pis
26 Cap	27 Pis	26 Pis	27 Tau	26 Gem	27 Leo	27 Vir	26 Lib	27 Sag	26 Cap	27 Pis	27 Ari
28 Aqu		28 Ari	29 Gem	28 Can	29 Vir	29 Lib	28 Sco	29 Cap	29 Aqu	29 Ari	29 Tau
30 Pis		30 Tau		31 Leo		31 Sco	31 Sag		31 Pis		31 Gem

WHAT YOUR MOON SIGN SAYS ABOUT YOU

Now that you know your Moon sign, read on to learn more about your emotional nature and your basic inner needs.

MOON IN ARIES

You have an emotional need to be first. And you want to be first *now*—there's no time to waste. Brimming with enthusiasm and energy, you love to keep busy and find waiting difficult. Remember to open up and talk to those closest to you about your feelings—they can help you to slow down and deal with any difficult emotions as they arise.

MOON IN TAURUS

You love to be surrounded by beautiful possessions and enjoy food and clothes that make you feel good—you have a need for comfort. Familiarity and routine are important to you, and you don't deal well with sudden change. That stubborn streak means you're able to stand up for yourself and protect your own interests, just remember to relax once in a while and try new things.

MOON IN GEMINI

Self-expression is one of your driving forces with this mix. Talking, drawing, writing—you simply have to communicate your feelings. And you love to listen to other peoples' ideas, too. To feed your curious intellect, you've probably got a tower of books and magazines at your bedside. Just don't forget to exercise your body as well as your mind.

MOON IN CANCER

You were born to nurture others—whether that's through baking them a cake or being at the end of the phone when they need your reassuring words. Family is hugely important to you, and you want to feel loved and secure. Being honest about this and accepting your wonderfully sensitive and emotional nature will help you find inner peace.

MOON IN LEO

You have an emotional need to be admired—all you really want is for everyone to love you. Your kind heart and generosity toward your friends and family means you are usually surrounded by others, and the attention you crave is easily won. When things don't go your way, you have a tendency to be dramatic—don't let your pride stop you from asking for help when you need it.

MOON IN VIRGO

You are a gentle soul and appreciate the simple things in life. Helping others in small ways makes you feel needed, secure, and purposeful. A clean and tidy environment is a must, and everything has to be in its proper place. Learning not to fuss when something isn't perfect is a challenge—look for useful ways to keep your practical nature busy and happiness will follow.

MOON IN LIBRA

Close bonds are everything to you—you find strength and stability in your relationships with others. Your need for balance and harmony means you are an excellent peacemaker, skilled at helping people to see and understand another's perspective. Remember to feed your love of beauty with regular trips to art galleries and picturesque places.

MOON IN SCORPIO

Deep and emotionally intense, you need to trust those close to you with your innermost thoughts and desires. All or nothing, you have incredible intuition and can see right to the heart of people. Finding one or two close friends who you can really open up to and be honest with about your feelings is important for your happiness. When this happens, your inner strength is unmatched.

MOON IN SAGITTARIUS

Your need for freedom and space is overwhelming, but when you achieve it, you are bright, breezy, and filled with a zest for life. Always on the lookout for new things to try and people to meet, your energy and enthusiasm lifts the spirits of those around you. Planning is not your strong suit; you prefer to go with the flow and see where it takes you—preferably somewhere fun and interesting!

MOON IN CAPRICORN

Ambitious and practical, you want to work hard and achieve results. You are conscientious and naturally organized, with a clear picture of what you want and how you intend to get there. Remember to take time to kick back and relax—the strong front you present to those around you can hide your more sensitive side. Letting go occasionally isn't a sign of weakness.

MOON IN AQUARIUS

Your desire to be unique and unusual is powerful, and you need the space and freedom to be yourself. Emotionally detached, you are happily independent and have an ability to see the bigger picture. Try not to lose touch with those closest to you—life is full of ups and downs, and friends and family can offer valuable support through tougher times.

MOON IN PISCES

Dreamy and intuitive, your sensitive nature is highly attuned to the feelings of others. Be careful to steer clear of negative people—you're likely to absorb their vibes, and they will bring you down. It's important you learn how to take care of yourself when you feel overwhelmed emotionally. Escaping into a good book or listening to your favorite music can be a great way to reset.

ELEMENTS

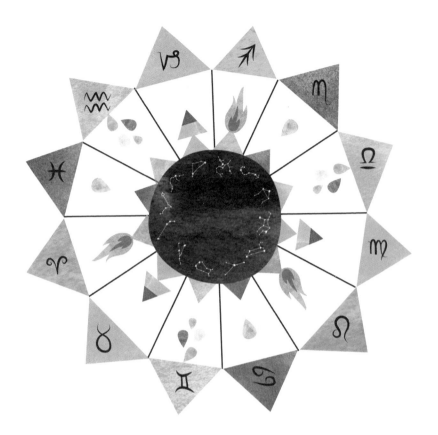

YOUR ELEMENTAL TYPE

Fire, Earth, Air, Water—in ancient times these were thought to contain everything that existed on Earth. Today that's no longer the case, but there's no denying their powerful effect on people's lives. Think of the heat from the Sun, the way earth is used to grow food, the water you consume, the air that you breathe. And like so much in astrology, each element has two sides. You drink water and rain helps plants to grow, but the force of a tsunami can wreak havoc and destruction. You have all four elements within you, but one or more of them will stand out. You could be a single type, or a mix of two or three. Your elemental type says a lot about you and those you interact with. When you meet someone you feel naturally comfortable with, it's often because you are elementally compatible.

IN YOUR ELEMENT

Aquarius is something of a contradiction in terms —a stable Air sign. You love to mix up the status quo, to take action against the predictable and outdated. A breath of fresh air, you are able to focus clearly and consistently until a solution is reached, and this gives you enormous creative potential. Although once you have made up your mind, nothing will change it. At your best you are innovative and free-thinking; at your worst you can be indifferent and aloof.

 AIR WITH FIRE

Air and Fire signs are wonderfully compatible—think of oxygen to a flame. You are full of ideas, and Fire is ready to put them into action. Together, you are a powerful, unstoppable force of activity. Remember, though, that relationships can become overwhelming if boundaries aren't put in place—Air has the ability to fuel Fire, but it can also blow it out.

 AIR WITH EARTH

Not an ideal mix. You want excitement rather than stability and can find Earth rather dull and dry, while Earth is irritated by your flightiness. You do challenge each other to think differently and see things from a new perspective, but together Air and Earth are more likely to create a dust storm.

 AIR WITH AIR

Like clouds drifting across the sky on a summer day, you really complement each other. Excitable and talkative, you both act on logic rather than emotion and love to share ideas and discuss things. Just try to be open with each other about how you're feeling, or your relationship may blow hot and cold.

 AIR WITH WATER

Your detached, objective thinking can leave Water thirsting for a deeper connection, but Air can also help Water to calm its emotional waves. But just like a can of fizzy drink, all those bubbles can cause an explosion when shaken or put under pressure.

THE MISSING PIECE

How dominant Air is within you depends on the influence of the other elements in your chart—ideally all four would be represented. Sometimes a lack of a particular element can cause an imbalance, making you feel rundown or stressed. The best way to counteract this is to tune in to the missing element and reharmonize yourself. Try the simple exercise below to get back in touch with any elements you're missing.

1. First, take a look at the Zodiac signs and their elements.

Fire: Aries, Leo, Sagittarius

Earth: Taurus, Virgo, Capricorn

Air: Gemini, Libra, Aquarius

Water: Cancer, Scorpio, Pisces

2. Now circle Air, as this is the element that represents your Sun sign. You're certain to have some of this element. Then do the same for your Moon sign and your Ascendant, circling the element associated with each.

3. Looking at the list, there should be one or more elements you haven't circled.

Fire—not enough Fire can leave you lacking in energy and motivation. You want to be more assertive and prepared to take the lead.

Earth—a lack of Earth can make you feel disorganized, off-balance, or like you couldn't care less. You might want more routine, structure, or to stay focused.

Water—with Water missing you may struggle to get in touch with your emotions or worry you're being insensitive. You're looking to express yourself, to feel more creative and inspired.

4. Choose the element you would like to tune in to, whichever one you feel might benefit you the most. Then pick one of the ideas from the lists below. If Earth is missing, you could take a picnic to the park and sit on the grass. If it's Water, you could try a soak in the tub. You can use this exercise whenever you feel out of balance.

FIRE

Sunbathe
Toast s'mores
Watch fireworks
Host a barbecue
Meditate on a candle flame
Catch the sunrise
Go stargazing

EARTH

Grow tomatoes
Pick wildflowers
Collect stones
Do cartwheels on the grass
Camp in the garden
Build a sandcastle
Roll down a hill

WATER

Spend a day at the beach
Splash in a puddle
Sit by a fountain
Walk in the rain
Catch a wave
Snorkel

We are
FAMILY

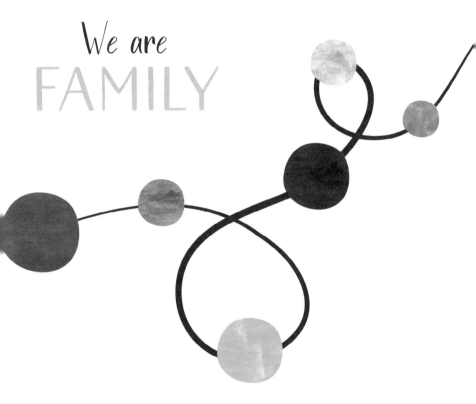

WE'RE ALL IN THIS TOGETHER

When so much in your life is changing, your relationships with your parents can become even more important. If you're lucky, you get along well with yours, but even the most harmonious relationships can come under strain during the teenage years. How can astrology help? It can remind you that parents are people, too. They might not get everything right, but hopefully you believe that they have your best interests at heart. Learning more about who they are, why they do things, and how you relate to them can make it easier for all of you to move forward together.

MOTHER MOON

The Moon sign you are born with can tell you a lot about how you see and treat your mother. This is because your Moon sign represents your emotional needs—what you need to feel safe and secure—and these are most often fulfilled by your mother. How you react to her can make a big difference to the way she behaves around you. If you are visibly upset by certain things she does, she is likely to change her behavior the next time around. If you react with happiness and delight, she is more likely to repeat them.

ARIES

You view your mother as strong, honest, and forthright. Sometimes, especially when she doesn't agree with your plans, this can make you feel as though she's taking over. Try not to push back too strongly, and remember she has your interests at heart.

TAURUS

You like to feel your mother is looking after all of your everyday needs and is dependable and reliable. Don't judge her too harshly if she doesn't always live up to your expectations—providing for others is often a careful balancing act, and she is likely doing her best.

GEMINI

Flighty and impulsive, you need your mother to give you the freedom to be yourself and make your own mistakes. Space and independence often have to be earned, though—what could you do to show her you're capable and trustworthy?

CANCER

Your longing for your mother's emotional attention can give you a wonderful bond and connection. However, the slightest hint of rejection from her can wound you deeply. Try not to take her reactions personally—it's okay for her to make choices and have goals that differ from yours.

LEO

You want to enjoy an open, honest relationship with your mother, where both of you say what you mean. Underlying this candor is a need for assurance and acceptance—when you feel vulnerable, be brave and explain to her how you feel.

VIRGO

You are aware of who gives what in your emotional relationship with your mother, and occasionally this can make you feel that she isn't there for you. Viewing her actions as "different" rather than "wrong" will help you to trust she is doing what she thinks is right.

LIBRA

You need your mother to recognize your emotional needs as valid and important. Try not to spend too much time putting others first—your relationship will flourish when you both accept the roles you play.

SCORPIO

You want your mother to respect your emotional boundaries and allow you alone-time when you need it. The trust between you can be intense and unconditional, so much so you may have to remind her to step back occasionally.

SAGITTARIUS

Upbeat and curious, your relationship works best when your mother is inspiring and encouraging, giving you the emotional freedom you need to expand your horizons. It's fine to chase independence, as long as you respect your mother's desire to give you roots.

CAPRICORN

You empathize strongly with your mother's feelings, so when she's struggling, this can make you feel it's your fault. Learn to let go of this guilt—it's unintentional and unhelpful. Instead, recognize how much you need each other's emotional support and encouragement.

AQUARIUS

You're not sure your mother's attempts to guide you are always necessary, and you don't like to burden her with your problems. Asking for help and talking things through might be more useful than you imagine and can bring you closer together at the same time.

PISCES

Your mother's high expectations have made you stronger emotionally, even though there are times when you just want to feel like a child and let her take care of everything. Taking responsibility can be tough; don't be afraid to speak up when you need support.

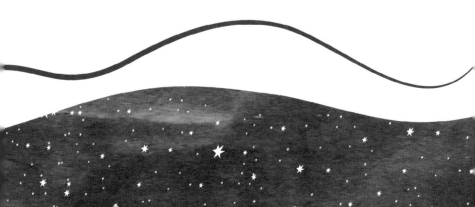

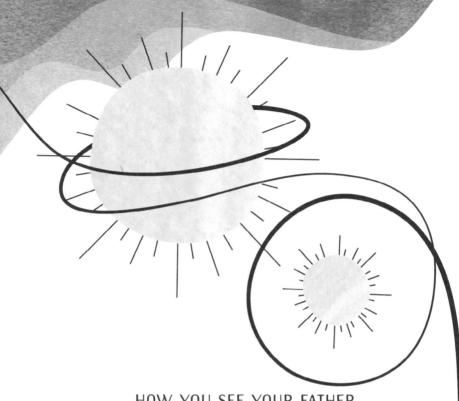

HOW YOU SEE YOUR FATHER

Just as your Moon sign gives you an indication of how you see your mother, or whoever plays that nurturing role in your life, your Sun sign can reveal the way you view your father, or the caregiver who is most involved with discipline. Your relationship with this person is built over time. For girls, it can have a strong bearing on how you view any future romantic relationships, whereas boys will either rebel or identify with these traits.

With your Sun sign in Aquarius, your father can sometimes seem unpredictable. While it's annoying, it means life tends to be exciting. He might find it hard to express his emotions toward you, but he demonstrates how much he loves you through his actions. So, he'll think about what you would love to do on a day off and then surprise you with the plan.

Now read on to find out how your father's Sun sign affects your relationship . . .

Your father's Sun sign will play a significant part in how you relate to him, and it can help you to understand why he acts the way he does—however infuriating it may sometimes seem!

ARIES

There's a push and pull in this relationship. You like to think about the long game, while your Aries dad often rushes ahead. Luckily, your shared view of the world at large helps to bridge the gap.

TAURUS

You may like springing surprises on your Taurus father and be hurt if he doesn't seem impressed. It's only because he likes to know absolutely everything in advance. Understanding this is key to clearing the air between you.

GEMINI

There's a meeting of minds in this partnership, and you rarely disagree. You're both determined to squeeze the most out of every day. Friends may even be jealous of how close you are.

CANCER

As a straight-thinking Aquarian, you might be puzzled by your dad's sensitive side. Why is he always so emotional? You both love to share, though, and this can help to open the lines of communication.

LEO

Your cool Aquarian nature is heated up by your father's warm personality, and you appreciate each other hugely. You might even head out on road trips together if you choose to indulge your shared love of travel.

VIRGO

When your kind natures combine, you're likely to volunteer for every charitable event around. While this is admirable, be careful to remember to include any siblings and other loved ones or there could be hurt feelings close to home.

LIBRA

More often than not you two are on the same page. And your super-quick exchange of thoughts and ideas seems to make you both think faster. Remember to include those around you, though, or they may feel left out.

SCORPIO

It's possible that you'll have your fair share of disputes because you are both headstrong. The good news, however, is that it's likely you'll end up admiring and even respecting each other, leading to a more settled relationship.

SAGITTARIUS

Equally able to see the bigger picture, the two of you can defuse any tense situation. Usually, you bump along together rather nicely, but if things do take a tricky turn, harmony and mutual respect tend to be quickly restored.

CAPRICORN

You could be the most organized parent/child combination in the Zodiac. At Christmas, you probably exchange planners for the coming year. If your dad can learn to lighten up, it could take your relationship to the next level.

AQUARIUS

Your Aquarius dad is young at heart—to the point that he's always asking about the latest buzzwords and bands. It can feel cringy, but he's likely to let up as the years go by—then you can start embarrassing the younger people in your life!

PISCES

Although you may not always see eye-to-eye, you frequently bond over a desire to help other people. This might include raising funds for local charities and events. Remember, though, to spend time with your nearest and dearest.

Best of
FRIENDS

FRIENDS FOR LIFE

Friends play an essential role in your happiness. They can help you to move forward when times are tough, see things from a new perspective, and encourage you just to have fun. Every good friend you make has different qualities that will influence you and allow you to make more of your potential. A friend might show you it can be better to hold back when all you want to do is rush in, motivate you to stick with that project right to the end, or inspire you to see an obstacle as a challenge. And astrology can be a great way to highlight those characteristics you're looking for in a friend. It can also tell you more about the type of friend you make for others.

WHAT KIND OF FRIEND ARE YOU?

You have lots of friends but only a few that you can count as close. For those privileged few you'll go to the ends of the earth. With the others, you're happy to flit in and out when it suits you, bringing excitement and fun into their worlds, but perhaps retreating if things get too heavy or you're not stimulated enough. You like your alone time, too. You rarely pass judgment on others, so your friendship group is wide and diverse.

Strengths: *Tolerant, independent, energetic*
Weaknesses: *Easily bored, rebellious, forgetful*
Friendship style: *Fun, exciting, unpredictable*

IF YOUR BEST FRIEND IS . . .

ARIES

Aries make friends easily. They're willing to help you achieve your goals, they see the best in you, and they're happy to take risks for you, too. They love to be someone's best friend and can find it difficult to feel second to anyone else. They are always on the lookout for new, super-fun adventures and are happy to take you along for the ride. They have a knack for bringing people from all walks of life together.

Strengths: *Loyal, generous, fun-loving*
Weaknesses: *Insensitive, demanding, petulant*
Friendship style: *Busy, fun, warm*

TAURUS

Considerate and charming, Taurus friends often have a talent for giving good advice. They like to take their time and allow friendships to develop slowly, but once you become close they treat you as a member of their family. As an Earth sign, they are dependable and grounded, and they make wonderful lifelong friends. Bear in mind they can place too much importance on material possessions, even judging others based on their wealth.

Strengths: *Caring, faithful, trustworthy*
Weaknesses: *Judgmental, stubborn, materialistic*
Friendship style: *Helpful, sweet, self-assured*

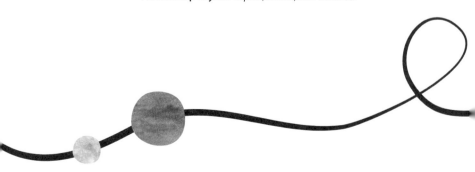

GEMINI

You'll need lots of energy to keep up with a Gemini friend. They love to have fun, do crazy things, and always have a story to tell. They'll make you laugh, but they can sometimes get a little carried away, perhaps exaggerating tales of their adventures in their effort to entertain you. They can be a bit gossipy, but they're not malicious. They're good listeners and will make you feel great, giving you lots of compliments—and always genuine ones, too.

Strengths: *Intelligent, energetic, fearless*
Weaknesses: *Impatient, easily bored, gossipy*
Friendship style: *Good listener, witty, spontaneous*

CANCER

Once you form a close connection with Cancer you have a friend who has your back. They're considerate and like nothing better than to make you feel happy. Watch out though; they're deeply emotional, which means that if you fall out— even over something small—you'll have to work hard to patch things up again.

Strengths: *Loving, caring, intuitive*
Weaknesses: *Unforgiving, anxious, sensitive*
Friendship style: *Warm, affectionate, protective*

LEO

As long as you don't expect too much from a Leo friend, you're in for a treat. Outgoing, confident, and full of energy, they thrive on social occasions and love to be the life and soul of a party, making people laugh and being admired. They're good at bringing people together and are in high demand, so you won't always have them to yourself, but if you can tie them down, you'll have some great quality one-on-one time.

Strengths: *Honest, brave, positive*
Weaknesses: *Arrogant, self-centered, proud*
Friendship style: *Supportive, cheerful, humorous*

VIRGO

With a Virgo by your side you'll always have somewhere to go when times are tough. They'll be there for you, giving you well-thought-out advice and a gentle sympathetic ear. Even when there's not a crisis, they're charming and kind. They like to be organized, so if they make plans, make sure you stick to them. They won't let you down, but they'll expect the same from you in return.

Strengths: *Warm, modest, smart*
Weaknesses: *Shy, serious, overly critical*
Friendship style: *Fixer, good communicator, reliable*

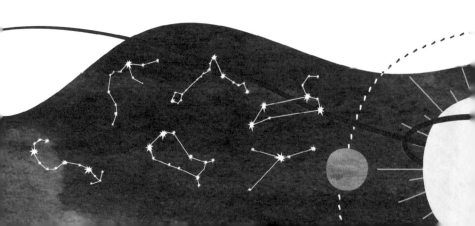

LIBRA

You can rely on your Libra friend to tell you how it is. They have a refreshing honesty, but they have a diplomatic way of sparing your feelings. They love spending time with you and like nothing better than a chat (especially if they're the one doing the talking!). They can always see both sides, so if there's a disagreement it won't be for long.

Strengths: *Diplomatic, honest, sociable*
Weaknesses: *Indecisive, people pleaser, chatterbox*
Friendship style: *Laid-back, devoted, forgiving*

SCORPIO

It's an honor to be a Scorpio's best friend. They're selective, so they don't always have many, but the friendships they do make will be really special. Once you've cemented your friendship, they'll open their inner circle to you and will want to spend lots of time together. In return, they'll expect 100 percent loyalty and might not take it well if you let them down, so tread carefully.

Strengths: *Passionate, hospitable, perceptive*
Weaknesses: *Guarded, jealous, suspicious*
Friendship style: *Intense, selective, highly loyal*

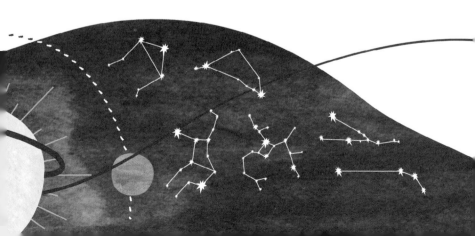

SAGITTARIUS

Sagittarius are low-maintenance friends. Easygoing, positive, and happy-go-lucky, they're up for anything. If you fancy an adventure, give them a call, but don't expect too much of them emotions-wise. Their friendship circle is wide and diverse, so you'll get to meet lots of interesting people, but they are easily bored and can struggle with emotional closeness. On the plus side, they won't put too many demands on you, so give them some space and enjoy the ride.

Strengths: *Adventurous, positive, open-minded*
Weaknesses: *Impatient, insensitive, easily bored*
Friendship style: *Generous, undemanding, never dull*

CAPRICORN

You might have to put in some groundwork, but once you've cracked the seemingly aloof exterior of a Capricorn you'll have yourself a genuine, warm, loving, and faithful friend. They'll show you complete devotion, through the good times and the bad. They're thoughtful and sensible and will know when to call it a night, but they will often surprise you with their sly sense of humor. They love to make you smile.

Strengths: *Responsible, supportive, faithful*
Weaknesses: *Condescending, standoffish, serious*
Friendship style: *Thoughtful, rational, work hard/play hard*

PISCES

A Pisces friend is a great listener who is sympathetic and caring and will always make time for you. They're the perfect friend if you need a shoulder to cry on, but they can sometimes get too emotionally involved. If there is any discord in your friendship, they are quick to blame themselves. Reassure them and let them know it's not their fault and you'll soon win back their love and support.

Strengths: *Loving, caring, good listener*
Weaknesses: *Sensitive, self-pitying, insecure*
Friendship style: *Supportive, sympathetic, selfless*

Your BIRTHDAY log

List the birthdays of your family and friends and discover their Sun signs

ARIES

March 21–April 20

Passionate, energetic, impulsive

TAURUS

April 21–May 21

Steady, tenacious, trustworthy

GEMINI

May 22–June 21

Intelligent, outgoing, witty

CANCER

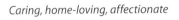

June 22–July 22

Caring, home-loving, affectionate

LEO

Loud, big-hearted, fun

VIRGO

August 24–September 22

Organized, modest, responsible

LIBRA

September 23–October 22

Charming, creative, graceful

SCORPIO

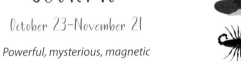

October 23–November 21

Powerful, mysterious, magnetic

SAGITTARIUS

November 22–December 21

Adventurous, optimistic, lucky

CAPRICORN

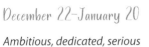

December 22–January 20

Ambitious, dedicated, serious

AQUARIUS

January 21–February 19

Eccentric, independent, imaginative

PISCES

February 20–March 20

Dreamy, sensitive, compassionate

Lucky in
LOVE

WHY OPPOSITES REALLY DO ATTRACT

The sign opposite your Ascendant (your Rising sign) on your birth chart reveals who you will attract, and who will attract you. Known as your Descendant, it's the constellation that was setting on the Western horizon at the moment and place you were born.

This sign is everything you are not—a kind of mirror image, or two sides of the same coin.

Yet, strangely, you are often drawn to the qualities of this sign over and over again in the people you meet. It's possible that these characteristics are ones you feel you lack yourself, and you sense that the other person can fill in what's missing. Sometimes it really is true that opposites attract!

Ascendant		Descendant
Aries		Libra
Taurus		Scorpio
Gemini		Sagittarius
Cancer		Capricorn
Leo		Aquarius
Virgo		Pisces
Libra		Aries
Scorpio		Taurus
Sagittarius		Gemini
Capricorn		Cancer
Aquarius		Leo
Pisces		Virgo

WHAT DO YOU LOOK FOR?

Once you've matched up your Ascendant with your Descendant from the list on the previous page, you can get to know the qualities that are most likely to attract you. You can use this information whether you're thinking about romance or friendship.

LIBRA DESCENDANT

You're looking for balance and harmony in your relationship, with someone who makes you feel interesting and important. You want to be listened to and value the ability to compromise. Gentleness and sensitivity are the qualities you're searching for.

SCORPIO DESCENDANT

You want an intense, passionate relationship with someone who will welcome you wholeheartedly into their world and want to spend lots of time with you. You are attracted to someone who will take control, but who will also look out for you and protect you.

SAGITTARIUS DESCENDANT

Adventure and fun are what you crave when it comes to love. You want someone open-minded who will accept you for who you are. You need to be given plenty of space to breathe and not be stifled by too many demands.

CAPRICORN DESCENDANT

You seek total dedication and devotion from those you love. You're happy to take your time and let a relationship develop naturally, and aren't put off by someone who appears cool or guarded. You like an irreverent sense of humor, too.

AQUARIUS DESCENDANT

You are attracted to someone who is independent and has a full life outside of your relationship, although you want to know that if push comes to shove, they will be right there for you. You like to be kept on your toes.

PISCES DESCENDANT

You're not afraid of a deep relationship with someone who wears their heart on their sleeve. You want to be cared for, emotionally supported, and loved unconditionally. You want to be the center of someone's world.

ARIES DESCENDANT

You like someone to spar with and who lets you have your own way, but is still strong enough to put their foot down when the gravity of the situation demands it. You will need to respect your partner's strength, bravery, and integrity.

TAURUS DESCENDANT

Stability and reliability are high on your list of priorities when it comes to forming relationships. You dislike chaos and are drawn to people who you know won't surprise or disappoint you. Instead you want a partnership that's grounded and safe.

GEMINI DESCENDANT

You're attracted to someone who is spontaneous and fearless, and who can keep you entertained. You're likely to fall for someone who makes you feel super-special and is quick to recognize your achievements and boost your confidence.

CANCER DESCENDANT

You seek relationships where you're made to feel like one of the family, where your every need and demand is met, particularly emotionally. You want to feel warm and fuzzy and protected by those you love.

LEO DESCENDANT

You're drawn to someone who is strong, confident, and outgoing with a busy social life but who can also give you warmth and passion when required. You're attracted to those who can make you laugh and sweep you off your feet.

VIRGO DESCENDANT

You long for kindness and tenderness in a partnership, along with reliability. You want someone who can bring order into your life and who will think things through in a methodical way. Nothing should be left to chance.

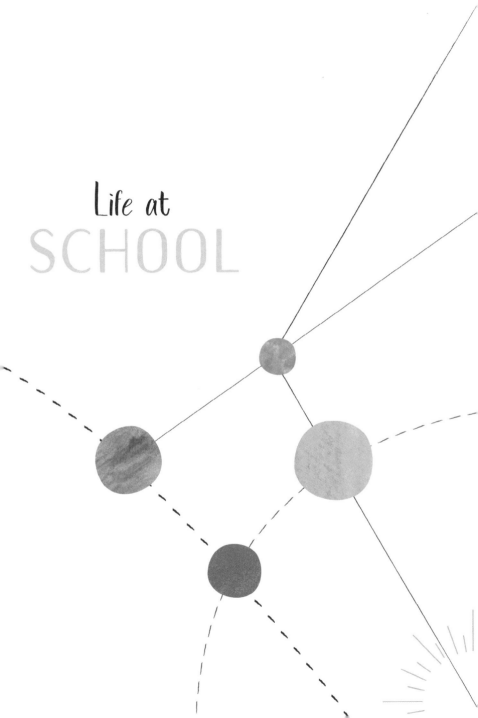

Life at
SCHOOL

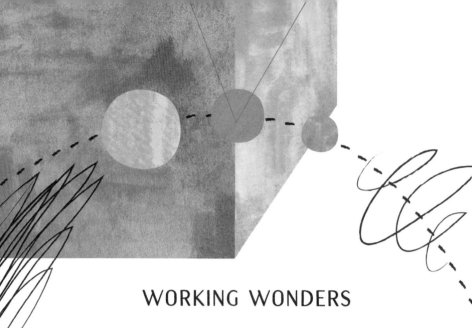

WORKING WONDERS

Have you ever been told that your years at school will be "the best of your life"?
Do you think they will be? Why? Many different things will determine how much
you enjoy your school days. And there are sure to be ups and downs along the
way. But there are a couple of important factors that astrology can help with. The
first is determining your skills and strengths, and the second is learning to work
well with others. Identifying your natural interests and abilities can help you to
develop a sense of purpose, and it's this that is most likely to motivate you to
work hard and actually have fun while you do it. To have a sense of purpose, you
need to know yourself and what it is you want from your life. Not what others
want for you, or what is expected of you, but what actually makes you come alive.

HIDDEN TALENTS

Not all of your attributes will be immediately obvious. Just because you're an
Aquarius doesn't necessarily mean you always feel detached, for example. You
can think about what a typical Aquarius might be good at, but you are unique,
and the stars are only a guide. Think about your strengths—both emotional and
physical. The examples on the right may strike a chord with you, or you might
want to create your own list.

BECAUSE YOU'RE ... AN OVERSEER

You are able to see the bigger picture. You are good at recognizing the important points in lots of information. You look at all the possibilities and narrow these down to the best.

Maybe you could be a ...
judge, environmental engineer, astrologer, life coach.

BECAUSE YOU'RE ... ANALYTICAL

You use facts and logic when making decisions. Ruled by the head rather than the heart, you are not easily swayed in emotional arguments. You are excellent with data.

Maybe you could be a ...
professor, scientist, social media marketer

BECAUSE YOU'RE ... OUTGOING

You are talkative and extroverted, and enjoy large groups. You can think on your feet and like to make quick decisions. You usually act first and think later.

Maybe you could be a ...
political activist, actor, sales person

BECAUSE YOU'RE . . . CREATIVE

You're full of ideas. You love to work imaginatively with ideas or designs and are good at coming up with new ways to do things.

Maybe you could be a . . .
fundraiser, artist, photographer, sculptor

BECAUSE YOU'RE . . . COOPERATIVE

You are prepared to compromise to get along well with others. You try to keep relations between others harmonious and help them to see differing viewpoints.

Maybe you could be a . . .
social worker, nurse, mediator

FAMOUS AQUARIUS PEOPLE

Virginia Woolf—*Author*
Oprah Winfrey—*TV host and activist*
Justin Timberlake—*Singer and actor*
Rosa Parks—*Political activist*
Yoko Ono—*Artist*
Cristiano Ronaldo—*Athlete*
Ellen DeGeneres—*Comedian*
Charles Darwin—*Naturalist, geologist, biologist*

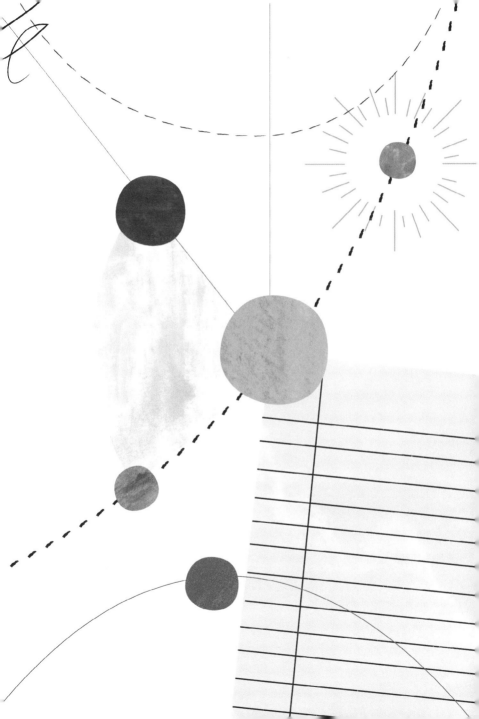

TEAM WORK

Working together with others is essential for almost any career path you choose to follow in later life. School can be competitive, yet working in collaboration with your peers rather than against them builds skills that today's employers are looking for.

Here's how well you work together with . . .

ARIES

While Aries takes the lead, you'll be happy to focus on the finer details. With your excellent problem-solving skills and independent thinking, you might come up with original ideas that will make all the difference, as long as they give you the freedom you need.

TAURUS

You two complement each other well. You're both happy getting down to the details and aren't bothered about being in the limelight, but while the bull is practical and well-grounded, you can look at the bigger picture and bring fresh ideas. The results can be remarkable.

GEMINI

The ideas will be flowing when you two sit around the table together, but make sure you don't get carried away. Someone's got to do the groundwork, no matter how mundane it might seem. The twins need to give you some space, and in return you must try to be more compromising. Get this right and you'll go far.

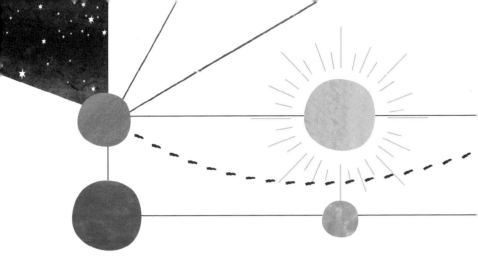

CANCER

You two have different priorities when it comes to what you want to achieve at work—and in life in general. Cancer wants emotional fulfillment while your priority is the bigger picture, but as long as you keep the lines of communication open there's no reason why you can't both get what you strive for.

LEO

You two can learn a lot from each other so that, as time goes by, your partnership will go from strength to strength. Leo can benefit from your wider vision while you can pick up some of Leo's people skills. Get this right, and it's a match made in heaven.

VIRGO

You both have a lot to bring to the table but don't always give each other credit. They need to recognize that you're bravely pushing boundaries. You need to remember that Virgo just wants to do things properly. Start appreciating each other's attributes, and you could be a force to be reckoned with.

LIBRA

Give you two a complex task and you're in your element. You're both Air signs, so you like nothing better than to get stuck into solving a problem or devising a new way of doing things, especially if it's for the greater good. Whether it's justice, equality, or another purpose, you both love fighting for the cause and, together, can make a real difference.

SCORPIO

You're both often misunderstood by those around you, but that doesn't mean you understand each other any better. The trouble is, you're both convinced you're right and find it hard to listen. You each have a lot to offer, but one of you will need to back down, just once in a while.

SAGITTARIUS

The ideas will be flying around the room when you two put your heads together, and they'll all be good, but therein lies your problem. Which ones do you choose? If you're able to decide (no, it won't be easy), take it through to the end and the results could be remarkable.

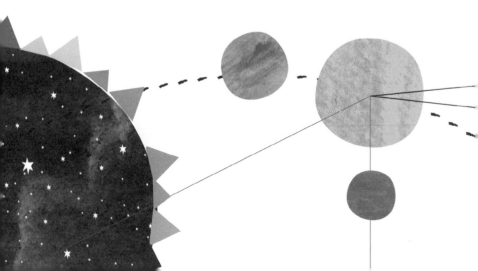

CAPRICORN

You come at things from opposing angles—Capricorn is motivated by their own professional standing and you by the world at large. If you end up in a team together, you must make sure you have a clear objective. If not, you're going to find it hard to get off the starting block, let alone see the task through.

AQUARIUS

With double the brain power, this team has excellent potential, but try not to overcomplicate things or aim too high. It's admirable to have all these big ideas, but you need to know your limits, too. Put too much pressure on yourselves, and your work might suffer.

PISCES

You might both feel a little underappreciated in this pairing, with neither side really understanding the other. Your aspirations are similar but don't quite match up: you want the world to be a better place, Pisces wants it to be kinder. If you're not careful, this can cause friction at times.

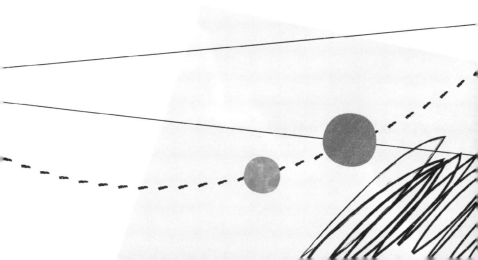

STERLING CHILDREN'S BOOKS
New York

An Imprint of Sterling Publishing Co., Inc.
1166 Avenue of the Americas
New York, NY 10036

ISBN 978-1-4549-3954-2

Distributed in Canada by Sterling Publishing Co., Inc.
c/o Canadian Manda Group, 664 Annette Street
Toronto, Ontario M6S 2C8, Canada

For information about custom editions, special sales, and premium and corporate
purchases, please contact Sterling Special Sales at 800-805-5489
or specialsales@sterlingpublishing.com.

Manufactured in China
Lot #:
2 4 6 8 10 9 7 5 3 1
08/19

sterlingpublishing.com

Design by Jo Chapman
Illustrations by Sara Thielker